Haiku Days of Remembrance:

In Honor of My Father

Also by Robert Epstein:

A Walk around Spring Lake: Haiku

(Editor) *Beyond the Grave: Contemporary Afterlife Haiku*

(Editor) *The Breath of Surrender:*
A Collection of Recovery-Oriented Haiku

Checkout Time is Noon: Death Awareness Haiku

(Editor) *Dreams Wander On: Contemporary Poems*
of Death Awareness

(Co-Editor with Miriam Wald) *Every Chicken, Cow, Fish and Frog:*
Animal Rights Haiku

Free to Dance Forever: Mourning Haiku for My Mother

Haiku Edge: New and Selected Poems

Haiku Forest Afterlife

(Second Author with Stacy Taylor) *Living Well*
with a Hidden Disability

(Editor) *Now This: Contemporary Poems*
of Beginnings, Renewals, and Firsts

(With Stacy Taylor) *Suffering Buddha: The Zen Way*
Beyond Health and Illness

(Compiler with Sherry Phillips) *The Natural Man:*
Selected Quotations of Henry D. Thoreau

(Editor) *The Quotable Krishnamurti*

(Editor) *The Sacred in Contemporary Haiku*

(Editor) *The Temple Bell Stops: Contemporary Poems*
of Grief, Loss and Change

(Editor) *They Gave Us Life: Mothers, Fathers & Others in Haiku*

Turkey Heaven: Animal Rights Haiku

What My Niece Said in My Head: Haiku & Senryu

Haiku Days of Remembrance:
In Honor of My Father

By Robert Epstein

2018

Published by Middle Island Press
PO Box 354
West Union, WV 26456

In Loving Memory
of
Corky

Table of Contents

Acknowledgments

As always, I want to thank family and friends for their love and support: Louise and Mel Adler, Kim Durham, Nancy and Norman Eisenberg, Martin Epstein, Rebecca Epstein, Clara Knopfler, Alyson and Anthony Nicolosi, Jane and Marc Parnes, Rocco Randazzo, Jay Schlesinger, Sophie Soltani, Lillian Schwartz,   Wendy Etsuku Siu, Stacy Taylor, and Miriam Wald.

I am indebted to Mel Adler and Lillian Schwartz for contributing Reminiscences of my father, which appear in two Appendices. Some of the poems in these pages have previously appeared in haiku journals that include: *Acorn, bottle rockets, Frogpond, The Heron's Nest, Mariposa, and Modern Haiku.* I wish to thank the editors again for including the poems in their publications.

I am very grateful to Ron C. Moss for his exceptional artistic eye and permission to use this striking image for the cover art. The old gas station pump reminded me of a time in which my father was young and passionate about cars—a passion that lasted a lifetime. Dad was also prone to superlatives, especially when talking about his inventions, such as the bidet, so I was thrilled to see "Super" appear in Ron's "Empty." Lastly, the image of a lone crow atop the gas pump couldn't be more perfect; its presence captivated me. My father loved to call back to birds that would break into song and would do so spontaneously as he labored intently under the hood of a car. Now, when I hear any bird sing or call, it is my father I hear, very close at hand.

Christina Taylor at Middle Island Press has done another exceptional job in bringing this book to print and I am filled with appreciation for her kindness and expertise.

Preface

Why not go out on a limb? That's where the fruit is.

~ Will Rogers

My father, Harry Epstein, died on Sunday, June 9th, sixteen years ago at the age of 78. Even after adolescence, when the upheaval of the 60s toppled most of my heroes, my father continued to loom larger than life. As a mechanical engineer, inventor, and all-purpose handyman, he appeared to know everything and seemed capable of doing anything. I think it is no exaggeration to say that, for my mother and siblings, Dad occupied *the* central place in our lives.

His death was, without question, earth-shattering for all of us. Despite my age, deep down in the bedrock of my psyche, I had unshakable belief my father was invincible. It was simply inconceivable to me that he could, or would, ever die.

Dad fostered this myth. Although his health had been declining, he was determined to undergo arduous back surgery so as to recover full use of his legs again, which had become increasingly unsteady due to scoliosis. As a man of fierce independence and pride, who thrived on grand visions, my father refused to live out the rest of his days in a wheelchair. He would have found that utterly unacceptable—an assault on his dignity.

It took a great deal of insistence as well as persistence, but Dad finally managed to recruit a cardiologist who would sign off on the back operation because his own cardiologist had significant reservations about the impact of such a procedure on his heart.

My father had hypertension and required bypass surgery some years prior. Around age 50, Dad had suffered a mild heart attack which he later dismissed as a heart attack at all.

My father underwent the grueling five hour procedure and, unsurprisingly, suffered a heart attack while on the operating table. Although he survived, the operation took a serious toll on his heart. Determined to get a third lease on life, as he had done following the previous bypass surgery, Dad scheduled the same procedure against the urgent pleas of my partner and me.

My father was undeterred. Shortly before he underwent the surgery, Dad said to me with unshakable conviction and resolve: "I've taken risks all my life." And so it was. This statement, I am certain, was the legacy my father wished to impart.

What my father shared with me during this phone conversation were the last words he ever spoke to me. Dad lived another ten days following the operation but his health and heart were severely compromised.

Dad was discharged from the hospital on Saturday, June 8, 2002. I asked my dear friend, Jay, to visit him and he kindly obliged, driving an hour and a half from his home in Chappaqua to Long Island, where my parents lived. Jay reported back to me that my father appeared weak but determined to recover. Before his surgery, Dad had told me that he had every intention of attending my younger brother's wedding that September.

It was not to be. Early Sunday morning, a nurse came to the house to check on my father, who had spent the night in his recliner. As the nurse took his vital signs, my father fell back suddenly into the chair, located in the recreation room that he had refurbished years before, and passed away at approximately 9 o'clock in the morning. The cause of death was later determined to be congestive heart failure. My mother, who was standing next to her *beloved Harry*, carried around guilt for many years because she didn't think to say "goodbye" to her dear husband of 55 years.

Following the shock of my father's death, all I could do was write. Between bouts of uncontrolled crying, I struggled to grab hold of as many images, memories, and associations as I could.

My sister and brother-in-law had recently sent me a birthday gift consisting of a sleek silver pen and several camel-colored journals. These became the vehicles for my mourning. On bereavement leave from work, I sat in a lawn chair outside the house and wrote and wrote for weeks. My primary mode of grieving was haiku. These mourning haiku enabled me to express my unspeakable sorrow, longing, love and anguish. As such, they were profoundly healing and therapeutic, though I didn't realize it at the time. In the face of my father's crushing death, I felt as though I was writing for my life; I didn't know what else to do.

On the second Sunday in June for the past sixteen years, I have dedicated a day in remembrance to honor my father's life. During the day, which I usually spend at one of my favorite parks, I write haiku that reflect his life as well as my time with him.

From an early age, I looked up to, and revered, my father. He seemed all-knowing and all-powerful. It wasn't until Dad turned my teenage world upside down by moving the family from New Jersey to Long Island that I stopped idolizing him. Our relationship became highly conflictual for many years after the move, which I regarded as a betrayal.

A turning point occurred in my late thirties, when I summoned the courage to write a letter to my father. In it, I confessed to him that, for years, I harbored the belief that he did not love me because I "failed" to live up to his expectations. Astonished, my father wrote a reply that started with an unprecedented apology as well as an explicit and unqualified expression of love. (See Appendix B)

This letter from my father paved the way for a reconciliation between us which was long overdue. Our relationship subsequently improved though, sadly, I didn't fully recognize, until my father's death, that I continued to carry with me a "frozen" image of him as self-absorbed and undemonstrative. With my father's death, the last vestiges of anger and resentment instantly melted away, and I was able to recognize, belatedly, the small gestures of affection he showed me in the latter years of his life.

As ironic as it may sound, I have grown closer to my father since he died. Immediately after my father died, I brought into my office a photo of him sitting in his iconic position (legs crossed, arm cradling his neck) because I wanted to include Dad in my daily work. Although I could not mention his death for several years without choking up, I have since made a point of referring to him with therapy clients whenever I found a compelling rationale for doing so. At other times, I invoke my father's spirit when I need guidance with a home or car repair. Doing so helps to center me enough to access the "mechanical mind" I need in order to figure out what I need to do.

Rationale

Why a book of haiku in remembrance of my father? Am I not, in effect, admitting that I have been unable to "get over" the death of my father, which occurred sixteen years ago?

I wish to straightforwardly address the bias in America, which persists despite the noble efforts of thanatologist, Elizabeth Kubler -Ross, more than fifty years ago, to bring death and dying, grief and loss, out of the shadows. Too many laypeople as well as mental health professionals continue to believe that mourning should be confined to a few months, at most, and when such grieving is "complete," the bereaved are expected to put the loss behind them and "move on" with their lives.

For some, such a path may work, and that is fine. I passionately maintain that each of us grieves in his or her own way and so self-healing will invariably look different for individuals. That said, I take issue, in general, with the notion that we must leave our loved one behind to be considered mentally healthy. I ardently contend that holding and honoring that loved one in our heart is no less healthy or adaptive. That is what this book is fundamentally about.

My father gave me life; for me, there is no more precious gift. Dad wasn't the most outwardly demonstrative or nurturing parent on the planet, but that was due primarily to his upbringing and not because he was unloving by nature. He provided for his three children and wife for his entire adult life and sacrificed much in doing so. I am eternally grateful to my father for all that he taught and gave me, and one important way for me to express my undying appreciation is by spending a day in remembrance each year on the occasion of his passing. Dad's death constituted a profound and long-lasting loss which the mere passage of time cannot undo.

More importantly, writing haiku in my father's memory on the anniversary of his death enables me to maintain the loving relationship which, in life, was complicated by our different temperaments, personalities and political viewpoints. The poetic perspective has a way of softening the edges of those differences, which I greatly value.

Writing haiku has allowed me to shape a home for memories that bring my father back to life. *In the realm of haiku, my father lives on.* How can this be? Haiku, rooted in essential qualities, create holograms that endure in the Eternal Now. Such is the miracle of haiku.

For one reason or another, I seem to suffer from the proverbial "bad memory." I stand in awe of others who have photographic memories that date back to toddlerhood. That is not me. Every recollection, however faint, is consequently invaluable to me. A good many poems in these pages consist of still photographs in my head that I have of my father. Others reflect qualities I associate with him that I found remarkable or worthy of mention.

Another rationale for a book of remembrance centers around wanting others to know who my father was. As the officiating rabbi said of my father during Dad's funeral service: "A good man's reputation lasts forever." My father *was* a good man, a loving husband and devoted father, so even though he had not achieved the kind of fame or fortune that he longed for, I want to introduce him to others. I have taken to heart what the French literary critic, Roland Barthes, remarked in *Mourning Diary* of his dear mother when she died: "Remember that she lived." I want to remember that my father lived, and I want others to know him, too.

Elaboration

I wish I could proudly say, with each passing year, the haiku written during the days of remembrance, have gotten deeper and more profound. Alas, this is not the case. The poems written in 2018 appear no clearer, poignant, or incisive than those written in the wake of my father's devastating death in 2002.

But poignancy and profundity are not, for me, the essential impetus for writing. In the grief over my father's passing, I was *driven* to haiku as a raw expression of my anguish and sorrow. I released both sadness and love through haiku. This was, first and foremost, the purpose of writing. Haiku was my primary mode of mourning.

No less important was the compelling need to preserve the lifelong connection I had with my father, imperfect though it was. My father served an immensely stabilizing role in my life. He had taught me so much, especially early in life, and I feel eternally grateful to him. In short, not only have haiku helped me to maintain an ongoing, loving relationship with my father, they enable me to honor his memory and celebrate his life.

Yet, there is something more: To the extent that haiku point us to our integral relationship with Nature, mourning or remembrance haiku situate my father's life-and death within the broader context of the natural world. Why does this matter? Insofar as my father's death is part of the natural way of things, haiku help me to *bear the unbearable.* Haiku is the poetic expression of love and truth, which enable me to keep my heart open and to hold onto my wholeness.

As I indicated above, I continue to write haiku about my father's life and death to remind me that he lived. In this way, I am inspired again and again to carry on with courage, integrity, and sensitivity until I take my last breath, just as he did.

Parental loss does not occur in a vacuum. Poetry, like every other form of human communication, is for sharing, as the late haiku scholar, William Higginson, asserted. Birth and death are universal experiences. In writing mourning or remembrance haiku which I can share with others who have also experienced loss (or eventually will), I feel less alone, less isolated, with my sorrow. For the past sixteen years, I have found myself uplifted after each day of remembrance simply by typing up the poems I write and e-mailing them to family and friends. I appreciate if someone takes a moment to write back, but it is not even necessary. I mainly want others to know that my father lived and although he is gone, he still matters to me; I still love him and always will.

Mourning or remembrance haiku, in short, are my way of nour-
ishing the shared heart that humanity needs if it is to survive. In
light of the many gifts I received from my father in terms of
knowledge, care and guidance, haiku transmutes all of this into
love, which becomes my responsibility to pass on. I do so with
deep gratitude to my father whose impassioned life as an inventor
enriched mine and, I believe, that of the human family to which
we all belong.

Robert Epstein
El Cerrito, CA
9 June 2018

Poems

2002

two surgeries
in four months
does Dad in

news of his death
staring a long while
at the blank sheet

my father dies
the half moon fades
from the morning sky

casket unseen
stroking my suit jacket
for comfort

crickets
w/o
my father

Half-Buried Treasure *

My Dad was not a religious man. He was born to Jewish parents of Russian descent, but they didn't practice the faith, either. Despite his lack of interest, he and my mother insisted that I attend Hebrew School, which I did twice weekly for seven years, while my friends played sports after school, until I was Bar Mitzvahed. The reason they required me to attend this religious training was because they didn't want to hear complaints from me in adulthood that they had deprived me of exposure to religious education.

Naturally, I hated Hebrew School. It was insufferably boring, as teachers relied almost exclusively on memorization, drills and quizzes, which I got in abundance five days a week in public school. So, it came as no surprise to anyone that I left the conservative congregation to which my parents belonged shortly after my thirteenth birthday, and never looked back. I was content, at that time, to emulate my father—who never set foot in a synagogue, nor spoke a word of Hebrew—and leave the world of Judaism behind.

In addition, I was rather angry at God. My parents decided to move not long after my Bar Mitzvah. the thought of leaving the beloved town I grew up in, and my growing circle of friends, shook me to my foundations. I prayed to God with all my might right up until the day the moving van pulled in front of our house and, when God failed to heed my wild cries for help, I wanted nothing more to do with Him. I finally found something on which I could agree with my father: there was no God. I didn't know why my father didn't believe in God; he either refused to answer my questions about his belief in the Almighty—which he did only weeks before he died—or he simply changed the subject, signaling that he had no interest in going there with me. In any event, I stopped believing in God in early adolescence, because no God I believed in would stand silently by as my world shattered around me.

It wasn't until my mid-thirties—call it a midlife crisis—when I rediscovered God, although I came to an understanding, with the help of meditation teacher, Stephen Levine, that God is beyond words, beyond comprehension. I conceive of God now as the force of Loving Intelligence in the world, though even this does not encompass God, fully, but it serves as a working definition.

In the past year, I reached out to God again through prayer, but the prayers have taken a softer, less desperate form. I asked God to guide my father during his illness and bypass surgery to peace, happiness, and freedom from suffering much in the Buddhist spirit of loving kindness, which mindfulness teachers have taught. These prayers are not rooted in wishful thinking, but rather an acceptance of suffering, which is inherent in human life.

I have also gradually come to reconsider the view that my father has lived an irreligious life. While he may have thought so, I no longer think this is accurate. Since his death, I have spoken to a cousin of mine who came with his parents to this country from Romania in 1962, when he was seven years old. My parents went to the port to greet this immigrant family when they arrived. My father, using broken Yiddish he had picked up listening to his father years ago, approached the new parents and asked, "Which one is your child?" He approached my cousin and presented him with a fire chief red Cadillac, with a little man inside. My cousin, who spoke no English, burst into tears, filled with gratitude.

But, that's not all. My father, who was the only relative at that time with a college degree, took it upon himself to help my cousin's father find a decent job, commensurate with his training as a chemist, in America. It was no easy task he had taken on, because my uncle didn't speak a word of English at the time. Undeterred, my father persisted in making his way through his sales network, searching for potential employers willing to take on a talented new employee. But, it was my mother, while reading the classified section of the paper, who found the lead that led to a pharmaceutical company where an old army buddy worked. My father took my uncle to the job interview, interpreted as best he could, and called in a favor. My uncle was hired, which enabled the family to obtain their own apartment in New York City and began a new life in the United States.

My father was not irreligious. His religion, I finally realized, as the Dalai Lama has said of his, was *kindness*.

After my father died a few weeks ago, I felt bereft. Although I have studied Buddhism and Taoism for many years, the words I found in books about emptiness, impermanence, the Unborn, sounded abstract and hollow to me. I searched for comfort but could find none anywhere.

My brother and sister privately prayed for a sign—any sign—that my father was all right. The morning after his funeral my mother woke up to find that her wristwatch had stopped and my sister walked into the bathroom that same morning to find the digital clock had gone blank. She said silently to herself: "Dad, if you're all right and are playing around in a new realm, then give me a sign by making the clock work again." And, much to her shock, the bathroom clock did start working again.

When she recounted this to me over the telephone, I said: "I wish that Dad could give me a sign too that he's all right, but I guess he can't be in New York and California at the same time. Maybe he's communicating through you to me." "I don't know," my sister said.

A few days later, I agreed to go out to dinner with my mate for the first time since Dad had died. I was standing near the front door of our house when I caught sight of something half-buried in our yard. I bent over, picked it up, scraped off enough dirt to see the last number of the date, which was "4." With that, I ran into the house, and poured hot water on the coin to rub off as much earth as I could. When I could clearly see the year of the quarter, which was caked heavily with dirt and must have lain buried in our front yard for years, I burst into uncontrollable sobs, knowing without question that my father had found his way to God, after all.

my father dies. . .

in the front yard a quarter

with the year of my birth

* From: *Haibun for Harry: Haiku Reflections in Honor of My Father*, unpublished, 2002.

Dad's gone
I ask my brother for
his impersonation

in mourning eight days are *one*

who I grieve for
is who I wish
to console me

deep sorrow
still the flowers
need watering

old frame
the letter my father wrote
I love you

morning light
on a post-it
he wanted me to go on

knock it off
Dad used to say
silence in life, in death

after his death
that affectionate squeeze
in his handshake

rush hour traffic
seen through the eyes
Dad gave me

sundown
I listen harder
for birdsong

rosebushes
given in condolence
chewed by deer

gone two months
longing to talk
or listen

missing Dad
tennis balls thump
against the backboard

sex ed class
the long ride home
with Dad

morning mail
a check for medical expenses
Dad's big signature

like Dad
I catch myself jiggling
change in my pocket

2003

Dad's only daughter
he never raised
his voice to her

in her Daddy's lap
she hurls a ball at Grandpa
ignoring her

raw pumpkin seeds
Dad never went
trick-or-treating with us

Father's Day
please tell me where
the fatherless go

sporting a buzz cut
and a cigar, Louis and Dad
brainstorm ideas (1)

Dad's reward
for making our beds
Corky!

at the bottom of my grief Dad's *goodness*

high school wood shop
the finely crafted bookcase
outlived him

Thanksgiving—
we wait for Dad to return
from the dead

2004

sketchy details
Dad's father let him spend
a night in jail

early on. . .
Dad listens to my cousin
and gives up smoking

made from scratch
the car my cousin built using
what Dad taught him

motorcycles—
Dad survived
to *forbid* me

four seasons:
when neighbors needed help
he's there

that heart attack
in midlife Dad managed
to minimize

first bypass—
the WW II vet finally
softens around the edges

Mom's sister
the hero she teased
and called Heschel

he answered
to my brother's nickname
Harold

living it
in black-and-white
Dad's death day

a day so calm
dozens of mechanical drawings
filed for posterity

Father's Day
I substitute
father sky

2005

to win me over
Dad builds a bedroom
in the basement

no one to talk to
I almost hug an old pine
Dad's death day

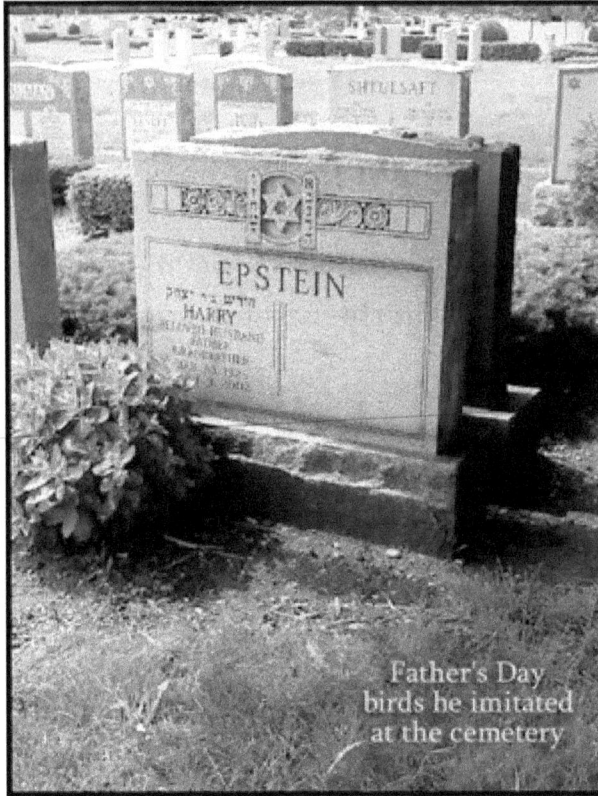

Father's Day
birds he imitated
at the cemetery

more quiet
than I can stand
Father's Day

in his boxers
nobody dared interrupt
the Sunday paper

don't block the road Dad's death day

watermelon spears—
it's deep summer and Dad is no more
than 40

2006

louder than him
a mockingbird kicks off
Dad's death day

gone four years
I put together
a collage of him

that restaurant out here
his childhood nickname
Eppy

nightly showdown —
on their bed Corky
growling at Dad

my friend as proxy
pays a call on Dad
the day before he dies

not
a visiting professor
Dad's death day

2007

five years later
realizing my father
died a *hero*

strong June breeze
praying for
my father's soul

stuck in traffic
drumming my fingers
the way Dad did

fifth death anniversary
my mother boxes up
a few more shirts

five years gone
that ride on his handlebars
five again

June 9th
looking for my father's face
in the clouds

fifth death anniversary
my father's watch
loose around my wrist

kicking a stone
he'd ask *what's new*
Dad's death day

the pen I used
to mourn my father
back in its gift box

Father's Day
I join the invisible
fatherless

Dad's workshop
I salvage the ice blue
stubby screwdriver

2008

the winter
Dad caught me
in a lie

bicycle horn
how many times
he fixed it

Dad came damn close
to striking water
summer drought

Dad's headstone
I saw him drunk
not once

hair down my back
he ordered me to cut it
but that's all

morning ritual
Dad had ample time
for fresh-squeezed juice

on my bike
in the rear view mirror
Dad's smiling face

2009

my father's birthday
his favorite songbirds
waiting for cake

Dad's 84th
how intently I listen
his outgoing message

medical supply store
pausing at a wheelchair
Dad might have used

Dad's up
the news is on
rise and shine!

in the garage
garden tools
older than me

too late . . .
in one ear & out the other
Dad's car knowledge

a day of remembrance
washing the car
the way he taught me

gone seven years
Mom lists the home repairs
my Harry should do

lost in thought
the same pose
as Dad

day of remembrance
I buy a pocket T-shirt
like those he wore

browsing the auto parts store Dad's death day

2010

death anniversary
I wake up and kiss
Dad's picture

fire chief's car
my cousin sends me Dad's gift
his death day

Father's Day
no better place
Home Depot

Father's Day
the time it takes
for tears to dry

Dad's legacy—
the bidet I still use
every day

using a tiny screwdriver

to tighten my glasses

Dad's hands *bigger*

unchanged

in his photo

gone eight years

gone eight years
Mom sits for a long while on
the edge of the bed

remembering Dad
the lamp timer
louder

gone eight years
atop his dresser
the to-do list

gone eight years
the side screen door
swings open

death anniversary
I thank my father
for giving me life

death anniversary
missing Dad's
superlatives

his last words
before surgery
I've always taken risks

the granddaughter
he never met also
bold and fearless

antique car show
I can't help looking
for him

Dad's death anniversary
tomato juice & crackers
for two

Dad's death anniversary
I contemplate a home
repair or two

Dad's death anniversary
on a meandering stroll
I ask a few hard questions

Dad's death anniversary
bringing his old watch
back to life

Dad's death anniversary
the way he curled
the garden hose

car grease
traces of it always
under his nails

the garage
a graveyard of mowers
Dad didn't get to fix

that guy
in cream loafers & plaid pants
could be my Dad

hall closet
Dad's younger granddaughter
trying on his hats

passing clouds
no trace of him this year
Dad's death anniversary

the way Dad
crossed his leg, cradled his head
cogitating

Dad's death anniversary
rereading war letters
to his Mom and Pop

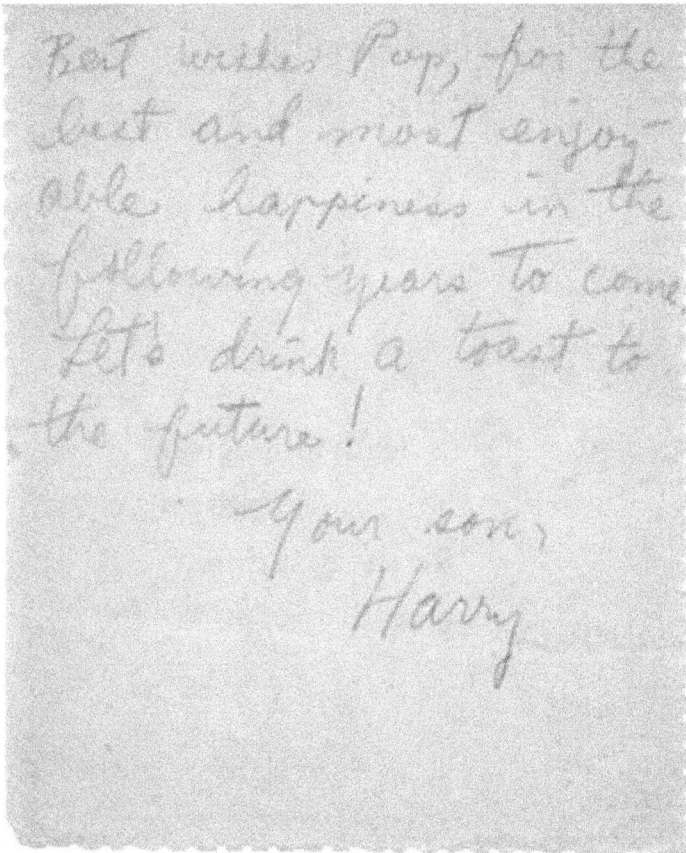

the pains he took
to conceal his pain
Dad's last days

Dad's death anniversary
I listen to his favorite music
for the first time

Dad's death anniversary
I dig out an old pocket knife
to clean my nails

years pass. . .
a growing resemblance between
our waist lines

Dad's death anniversary
rolling up my shirt sleeves
before dinner

a sudden spill
I learned to curse that way
listening to Dad

Dad's death day
I pray to the God
he didn't believe in

another
sundown
w/o
my
father

2011

Marilyn Monroe
as naked as summer grass
Dad's dark workshop

beyond
the tallest mountain
Dad's death day

the way Dad ran
pine through the electric saw
9 years gone

my peer
Dad's rusted
red gas can

here I am
whenever you tie your laces
Dad's death day

walking
in the next aisle
Dad's old cap

He's back! He's back!
the mockingbird sounding
too eager

Dad's death day
shaped by church bells
ringing

Dad's death day
closing my eyes
I'm cradled again

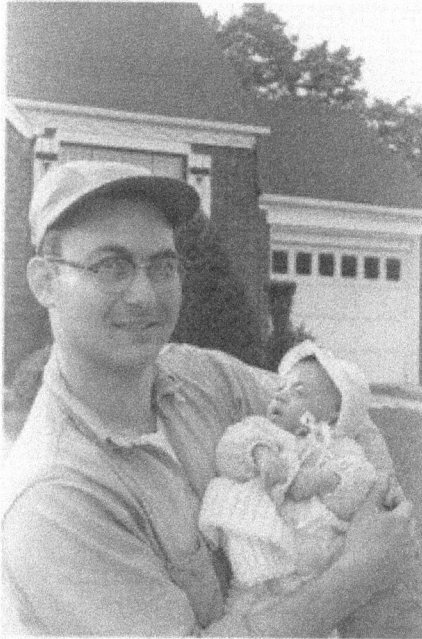

two thumbs up
from a passerby
Dad's death day

a little slower
with a mechanical pencil
Dad's death day

w/o sunglasses
it's a different gravesite
Dad's death day

across the field
no one answers the phone
Dad's death day

trudging
the sound gravel makes
Dad's death day

seeking refuge
behind a young shrub oak
Dad's death day

nothing worth
staying closed to
Dad's death day

in his honor
tonight I eat my peas
w/o the smirk

WW II bomb squad
surviving, so he said
w/o god

57
and
miss
ing
my
father

dry creek
the fatherless
need a day

day of remembrance
a wild pheasant appears
w/o Dad

country drive
my first published haiku
Dad stares blankly

two blue jays
one of them reminds me how
Dad dressed for work

the way
an emptied vase
still holds my grief

commemorative
candle
blown
out
by

god
knows
what

closing my eyes
I see Dad's lathered face
and his steel razor

in the days
before A/C. . . Dad's left arm
tanner than his right

multi

plying

9

times

365

days

missed

nine years gone
I'll have what he's having
Dad's death day

letting the late sun
open my rib cage
Dad's death day

he could laugh
but didn't joke
Dad's death day

when did I substitute
dinner for *supper*
Dad's death day

Dad's death day
writing one last poem
in the June air

larger than life
Dad's signature
Father's Day

cemetery walk
the lament in that flute
Father's Day

socks
that can't be darned
Father's Day

a distant siren
breaks the silence
Father's Day

2012

burning leaves
in the backyard
Dad Dad Dad

gone ten years
I look for my Dad among
fallen pine needles

gone ten years
Dad never talked about
his parents

Father's Day
how time moves
w/o one

Father's Day
for a while I palm
his stubby screwdriver

a half-blue sky
so many unfinished projects
Dad's death day

birds scattering
Dad never asked
for directions

gone ten years
Dad never took us
camping

the air a little thicker Dad's death day

a young girl calls
from her lemonade stand
Dad's death day

nothing to fix Dad's gravesite

vibrate only
Dad would be using
a smart phone

his message says
he'll return your call ASAP
gone ten years

he last kissed me
I reckon
fifty-four years ago

in pine shade
remembering Dad
never sat much

like a speeding bullet
Dad's response
to car trouble

missing him
I wax the car
Father's Day

baby pictures
I'm not the only one
who looks sleepy

old sequoia
Dad's presence
was *that big*

---

remembering Dad
I cross paths with
a monarch butterfly

gone ten years
yet Dylan says
death is not the end

Dad's death day
laying to rest
the camera he bought me

Dad's death day
he taught me
how to ice skate

this time
the siren's for someone else
Dad's death day

three dots
for his unfinished life. . .
Dad's death day

a caw
I can't comprehend
Dad's death day

. . . haven't fixed
a bike flat in years
Dad's death day

37 years vegan
he never took me fishing
Dad's death day

meditating
in the hospital lobby
Dad's still dead

Dad's death day
I don't believe I know
his favorite drink

starless night
but for one brief twinkle
Dad's death day

back again
the father I remember
by birdsong alone

~ *after Paul O. Williams*

Dad's death day
I say goodbye to a few
more strands of hair

July 4th
amid the booms
Dad's absence

2013

Dad's death day
opening my eyes
on the out-breath

Dad's death day
only spiders use
his tools now

Dad's death day
the boy he was
stares back at me

Dad's death day my back goes out

age spots his hands
age spots my hands
Dad's death day

through the cold
a stream of warm air
Dad's death day

my fondest memory?
arms around his neck as Dad
swims to the buoy

Dad's death day
a snowy egret
bone-still

that different hue
after the fog burns off
Dad's death day

gone eleven years
the padlock to Dad's shed
frozen shut

raking crabapples
all the things he taught me
Dad's death day

did he ever sing Dad's death day

listening for echoes
in the children's park
Dad's death day

Dad's death day
meditating
the end of time

ever so slightly
the park swing sways
Dad's death day

Dad's death day
comes and goes
I am a rock

Dad's death day
what I remember
floats away

Dad's death day the shadows

the near-fights
over Mom's fries
Dad's death day

Father's Day
in the fortune cookie
nothing

2014

house finches
briefly dot the sky
Dad's death day

children's park
a yellow balloon pops
Dad's death day

I used
to stroke his arm hair
Dad's death day

the way June died
twelve years ago
Dad's death day

fog *Dad's* fog
fog *death* fog
fog *day* fog

no chrome
to polish on my car
Dad's death day

'58 Edsel
if there is a heaven
he's driving again

brown hillside
I still remember
my father's voice

robin's nest
when Dad died
I fell out

park bench
I slide over a little
Dad's death day

gone 12 years
the crickets know it
and say so nightly

buckets of screws
Dad was prepared
for everything

condolence bush
sliding it closer
to the light

gone 12 years
Dad's spot
still vacant

starched white shirt
I wear it for him
Father's Day

Father's Day
unlit
Dad's barbecue

2015

Dad's death day
blue drops of rain
begin to fall

Dad, are you there?
that red cardinal
in the branches

for the love
of hummingbirds
please come home, Dad!

the lagoon
shallower this summer
Dad's gone 13 years

beyond hope
a great blue heron faces me
Dad's death day

Canada geese
that don't stop honking
Dad's death day

not a boat
moving in the Bay
Dad's death day

the rough surface
of that picnic table
Dad's death day

tall grass
so dry it hums
Dad's death Day

eucalyptus
where the nature walk ends
Dad's death day

Dad's death day
all Mom can say
I love you

hat shop
I look for one he might like
Dad's death day

Howard Stern
chases his staff
Dad's portable bidet (2)

hillside acacias
we share a place in the sun
Dad's death day

I buy one more tool
I will never use
Father's Day

that's the spirit!
a grey water car wash
Father's Day

aimless bike ride Father's Day

no one
on the handlebars
Father's Day

2016

the heights
that hummingbird attains
Dad's death day

meditating
a wind blows through me
Dad's death day

shadows converge
on his headstone
Dad's death day

new used car
I ask his opinion
Dad's death day

another year
closer to my departure
Dad's death day

how he thought
with his index finger
Dad's death day

reading haiku
the engineer tries to grasp
Dad's death day

he had no time
for the stock market
Dad's death day

Sunday drive
to look at houses
Dad's death day

no overt advice
on navigating the world
Dad's death day

cars cars cars
mostly his world
Dad's death day

he could repair
just about anything
Dad's death day

realizing too late
brake jobs were the way he loved
Dad's death day

tennis court—
he drove himself to the ER
Dad's death day

no way
a motorized wheelchair
Dad's death day

after the bypass
he went meatless too
Dad's death day

how he insisted
I never get depressed
Dad's death day

the boy in him
back on the tennis court
Dad's death day

Haiku Days of Remembrance: In Honor of My Father

fog burning off
will I see you again
Dad's death day

gadgets gadgets gadgets Dad's death day

180

if only
I could show *this* to him
Dad's death day

his college ring
still too big
Dad's death day

if he could
then I can try
Dad's death day

Father's Day
I give myself
a good talking to

2017

Passover
Dad never disappeared
for days

before there was light Dad's death day

gone 15 years
Dad and I closer
to a reunion

the inventor's son
has an idea too
Dad's death day

my parents
lying together again
Dad's death day

still irreplaceable
after 15 years
Dad's death day

Mom's absence
deepens the void
Dad's death day

morning walk
leaving no footprints
Dad's death day

roaming the streets
for something to salvage
Dad's death day

early bird Sunday
I invite him to supper
Dad's death day

I'm here
he's there
Dad's death day

the garden
shaped by a ghost
Dad's death day

how quickly
dust accumulates
Dad's death day

a cardinal sings
3,000 miles away
Dad's death anniversary

another shoot
on the tree stump
Dad's death day

with John Henry
he lived by the hammer
Dad's death day

slower
than that box turtle
Dad's death day

his heart
my heart
Dad's death day

you won't find him
in these three lines
Dad's death day

Dad's death day
I pump up
the bicycle tires

gone fifteen years
I reinvent him
for Father's Day

2018

June 9th
Dad dies again
for the 16th time

I close my eyes
to awaken him
Dad's death day

missing Dad
I reorganize
my desk drawer

more rain
straighten up the garage
Dad whispers

sometime
after midnight Dad drives up
in his *dreamcar*

well into old age
still under the car fixing
God knows what

depression?
not him not
on your life

professional baseball
the first of many
sacked dreams (3)

backyard pool
Dad's splash
bigger

Sunday afternoon
playing catch with Dad
the smell of new leather

teaching us tennis
once in a while Dad lets loose
a lightning serve

Dad's reward
after mowing the lawn
Mom's lemonade

crying only once
his middle sister lowered
into the ground

in stark contrast
to his freewheeling work desk
Dad's sock drawer

Today's Bidet
Dad pitches it
to Muhammad Ali (4)

Muhammad Ali
tickles his ear
Dad's death day

Dad loved to talk
around the coffee table
Planter's mixed nuts

father & son bowling
not even juvenile arthritis
gets in the way (5)

chili peppers
I don't remember him asking
what's wrong, son?

winter rain
the auto repair moves
to the garage

Dad as a boy
there is ingenuity
in those eyes

during the war
and after his heart attack
Dad's *mustache*

Dad's first of its kind
do-it-yourself auto repair shop
closes

Dad's leg
flung over the recliner
the late night news

snowy night
Dad fixed the broken-down car
despite his heart attack

not so much
an outdoorsman
Dad under the hood

summer chirping
Dad in his castle
me in my treehouse

Dad could fell trees
but vegetable gardening
not his thing

Dad's invention
but I just learned how
to tie my laces! (6)

IT'S SOOOOO EASY!

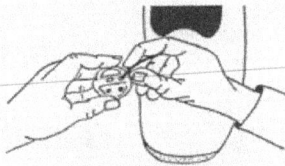

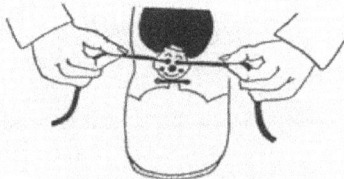

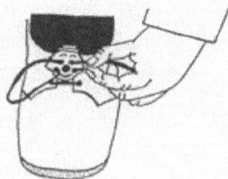

for a patriot
Dad never displayed
the flag

stretching his back
Dad always let Mom
do the complaining

stop your bellyaching
the one who spoke those words
long gone now

that creaking
could be nothing
Dad's death day

Crestwood Lake
small enough to swim
on Dad's back (7)

nothing to stop us. . .
a spin in his T-Bird dreamcar
haiku afterlife

birds scattering
Dad never asked
for directions

one blossom
is all it takes
Dad's death day

ending it
with a burger & fries
Dad's death day*

*Vegan burger, that is

it could be so
a lone crow brings word
Dad's death day

Notes

1. As a child, my father would take me with him for a brain-storming session with his good friend, Louis Duz. I believe they may have met at the Ford plant where both worked. When they got together in Louis's living room, Louis would throw out ideas for products that my Dad would design, if he thought them feasible and marketable.

2. Believe it or not, my father also managed to get on Howard Stern's radio program in hopes of increasing bidet sales by persuading the shock-jock's listeners to take their rectal hygiene to the next level. Howard ended up chasing staff and spraying them with the working bidet that my father brought with him. To the best of my recollection, there was no ongoing spike in sales following the Howard Stern stint.

3. Like many young boys, my father aspired to become a professional baseball player. Alas, it was not meant to be: The need for prescription glasses in high school dashed those dreams. Instead, with the outbreak of World War II, Dad enlisted in the army and was shipped to France, where he was the youngest member of a bomb disposal squad.

4. In my father's indefatigable efforts to market his beloved bidet, which he hoped to see in every bathroom in home and hospital, he reached out to none other than Muhammad Ali, hoping that the World Champ would convince Muslims to buy his product. Alas, it was not to be, but Dad did come away with a photo of Ali, his agent and my father (far right).

5. My younger brother was diagnosed with childhood onset arthritis. Still, he and Dad enjoyed Sunday bowling with a local league for a number of years.

6. One of my father's early inventions was the *shoelace script*. It was intended to eliminate the inconvenience of needing to tie one's shoelaces. Dad had grand plans to use the image of Ronald MacDonald as well as the faces of the Beatles. He wanted me to wear the shoelace scripts to school, but I was too embarrassed to.

7. Crestwood Lake, located in Ridgewood, NJ, was the highpoint of the summer for me, as the family would spend the day swimming and eating a picnic lunch packed with peanut butter sandwiches, potato chips and chocolate milk. *Those were the days.*

Appendix A: E-mail to My Father

Date: June 1, 2002 10:07PM

Subject: EXPRESSIONS OF GRATITUDE

Dear Dad,

Hi. I was saddened to hear that you are in so much pain, feeling like you're hanging by a thread, as you put it. I wish there was some way that we could ease your pain, wave a magic wand and speed up your recovery, but you've been on this planet long enough to know that Life doesn't work that way. So, you are faced to take the long route back to health.

The only thing I know how to do when I'm feeling a lot of feelings is to write. You've been on my mind a lot and, although we're not accustomed to sharing feelings, I want to do so in any event. I hope you will indulge me!

I think what I most wish to convey is my gratitude. I've been reflecting on what you've taught me—most of which dates so far back that, like you, I have only fuzzy fragments of recollection—but these are some of the things I remember:

* thank you for teaching me how to tie my shoelaces
* thank you for teaching me how to color coordinate my clothes
* thank you for teaching me how to organize my drawers (which I learned by looking through your drawers. Stacy has always been impressed by the "neat appearance" of my drawers.)

* thank you for teaching me how to throw and catch a ball and for playing catch with me though you had lots of other things to do
* thank you for teaching me how to use some very basic tools, like the hammer, screwdriver, electric drill, various wrenches, saw
* thank you for teaching me how to sand and remove paint
* thank you for teaching me how to paint with brushes and with a roller
* thank you for teaching me how mow the lawn, which I loved to do
* thank you for teaching me how to burn leaves, which I also loved doing (though not the raking so much!)
* thank you for teaching me how to change a flat tire on my bicycle
* and thank you for taking me for bike rides, which are some of my fondest memories
* thank you for showing me how to build model cars and airplanes and for coming to my rescue when, as often happened, I got exasperated trying to read instructions I could never comprehend
* thank you for exposing me to other hobbies like woodburning and the jigsaw, with which I loved making doorstops and napkin holders, which I hand-painted and was very proud of at the time
* thank you for teaching me how to swim at Crestwood Lake or Rockaway, where I have some of my sweetest memories of all playing in the water and eating Cheetos and peanut butter sandwiches that Mom prepared
* thank you for introducing me to musical instruments, even though I don't feel I had a musical bone in my body!

* thank you for teaching me how to play ping pong, which I still love to this day, although I haven't played in a long time
* I'm pretty sure you taught me how to ice skate and for this I am deeply grateful to you, since I had countless hours of pure pleasure and joy skating, which I took up again out here until I started having back problems
* thank you for teaching me how to take my education seriously
* thank you for teaching me the importance of helping one's neighbors, which I learned by watching you help our neighbors, both in Saddle Brook and in Seaford
* thank you for teaching me the value of money
* and thank you for teaching me the value of mending broken things, which I learned by watching you resurrect discarded objects like the swing that still hangs on your front porch
* thank you for teaching me sound moral values, like honesty and respect for one's elders
* thank you for teaching me how to drive at the ripe old age of 16 and for investing countless hours of blood, sweat and tears to get my first car, the '64 Valiant that Claire and Paul gave me, up and running
* thank you for doing countless repairs on the succession of used cars I drove after the Valiant; I can't even begin to add up all the brake jobs you did and water pumps you replaced, but I offer one BIG THANK YOU for all of them!
* thank you for teaching me how to buy and sell used cars, which can be very intimidating to anyone—like Stacy—who hasn't done so before

* thank you for introducing me to Sigmund Freud, whose collected writings was in one of the bookcases at home, though I'm sure you had no interest in him whatsoever!
* thank you for showing me by your own example that it was possible to leave a job to start your own business, that you valued self-employment, which gave me inspiration to pursue a part-time private practice in psychotherapy
* thank you for all your loving concern and support over the past several years with the health problems that Stacy and I have experienced. You have no idea how much this has meant to both of us, who can get so overwhelmed and discouraged
* most of all, I want to thank you, as I have said, for demonstrating to me the vital importance of persevering despite confusion, overwhelm, and discouragement. The very health crisis that you are presently living through is perhaps the most important teaching of all, and I shall not soon forget the great courage you have displayed, even though you may not think it's courage at all: every family knows differently

Well, I've probably exhausted you by now with this long list. If I had more time and a better memory, no doubt the list would be much longer. Tonight, in Borders [Bookstore], I was glancing at a book and came across a story that I want to share with you. Two mothers were talking while their daughters played nearby in the garden. One of the 5 year old girls told the other that her grandfather had recently died and she didn't want to forget him because he went to God in heaven. The other girl politely disagreed with her friend, saying that her grandfather didn't go to heaven to be with God, because God is right here, pointing to her and her friend's heart, and even in the flowers.

I want you to know that, as God exists in my heart, so too will you. Always. There is a loving kindness prayer that I wish to say for you, and for Mom:

May you be happy,
May you have peace of mind,
May you be free of pain and suffering.

Love,

Robert

Appendix B: My Father's Letter to Me

My Dear Son Robert,

This is truly a momentous occasion...I can't remember when I last
sat down to write a personal letter. I don't think I EVER wrote
to you! Sorry about that. There just doesn't appear to be enough
time for such personal luxuries...sounds like a familiar lament...
doesn't it?

In any event, I must admit that your letter truly touched a sensitive
nerve or two! It even caused a large lump in my throat which isn't
really too easy to do. However, to start with...let's have a strong
BEAR HUG and maybe even a kiss! If you were here, that's what I'd
insist on doing right off the bat!

In addition, if there's even a doubt, or just a suspicion...you HAVE
to know that I LOVE YOU VERY VERY MUCH!! And I have always loved you.
I realize now and I hope not too late...that perhaps I didn't convey
that feeling convincingly enough. My entire youth and upbringing
consisted of very undemonstrative emotions...especially regarding
love. There were NEVER open expressions shown! This invironment
has plaqued me throughout my entire life...from my relations with
mother and now, unknowingly, with you until now.

I, wholeheartedly, grasp this opportunity to correct your misconcept-
ion of my true feeling toward you. I repeat...I love you VERY VERY
much...as I   always have...since birth!

I am also VERY VERY VERY PROUD of you...your accomplishments, both in
your education and career pursuits and more so as a MAN! I have al-
ways admired your courage to stand behind your convictions...even if
they were unpopular. Your strength, fortitude and endurance during
the lean years of acquiring your education has been a constant source
of enormous pride to me...and also a great deal of personal pain and
sorrow on my part...for not being able to help you out financially,
as I have longed to do.

If I hurt you during your "growing up" years...I apologise. What more
can I say? I did what I thought was right...at the time. I really
don't know if I'd repeat the same things today...it's had to say...
I'm not really the same person...or maybe I am?

In any event, let's get on with the living! Time's too short for
dwelling on the past! I'd like to think that recognition of our past
tribulations only insure a stronger, healthier and more productive
future! Let's raise a toast to yours..DOC!

I anxiously look forward to a personal get-together so that we can
further cement our relationship!

Love,

DAD

Appendix C: Prayer to My Father

MY PRAYER:

DEAR DAD,

MAY YOUR SOUL BE AT PEACE,

MAY YOUR SPIRIT BE FREE,

MAY YOUR HEART BE FILLED WITH LOVE AND JOY,

AND

MAY YOUR MIND BE ACTIVE AND CREATIVE, ALWAYS.

DEAR GOD,

PLEASE HEAR MY PRAYER FOR MY FATHER,

AND LIBERATE HIM FROM

THE WHEEL OF BIRTH AND DEATH,

SO THAT HIS SOUL MIGHT BE FREE OF SUFFERING

AND LIVE IN THE LIGHT

OF YOUR ETERNAL LOVE, FOREVERMORE.

AMEN

Appendix D: Lillian Schwartz's Reminiscence of Her Brother-in-Law

My earliest memory of Harry Epstein goes back to his first date with my sister, Evelyn. We lived at 110 West 83rd Street, one flight up to our apartment. The date was arranged by 3 sisters, friends of the family, and when Harry rang the doorbell I was sent downstairs to open the door for him. I think he was in uniform, World War II was on, and I seem to remember his removing his hat while walking upstairs behind him. I guess Evi and Harry hit it off because they kept in touch. I must have been about 9 years old. Harry gave me his soldier's address and we wrote to each other while he served his country in Europe. I saved his letters for years and I now regret my decision to throw them out after a big closet cleanup. However, I have a few photos taken in Central Park on one of his visits.

Our family moved to 48 West 83rd Street, a spacious 5-room apartment closer to Central Park. When the war ended, Harry started dating my sister and he always drove up in what I think was a 1939 coupe, stick shift, with an open back seat for two. I always whined when he came in...."Harry, take me for a ride," and good scout that he was, he drove me up and back Central Park West before getting his date started with Evi. I was thrilled as my father did not own a car. While Evi was getting ready for a date, Harry and I sat in the living room and I was able to talk to him like a big brother about anything and everything and he always gave me good advice. When I was 16 I wanted a bike badly and was disappointed when my parents gave me a birthstone (Garnet) ring instead. But Harry showed up with a bike from parts he made himself for me and I was thrilled. One weekend my girlfriend and I biked to Palisades Park in New Jersey but after enjoying the park rides our backsides were so sore we could not sit on the bikes. Harry came to our rescue, somehow attached the two bikes to the back of his car, and drove us home.

He was a wonderful brother-in-law to me as a kid and as an adult, and I know he and my sister enjoyed a happy marriage through the years they were together.

Appendix E: Mel Adler's Reminiscence
of His Father-in-Law

Harry Epstein (Hebrew: Herschel) was my father-in-law; he had no choice. I had dated and eventually married his only daughter, Louise, and was warmly welcomed into his family.

As luck would have it, Harry and I shared similar interests and over the years that followed, we often collaborated on automotive and home repair projects, on sales and marketing ideas, which we openly debated at every family gathering.

His memory still lives in every classic car we see or songbird call we hear and... With every special tool that I still borrow from his massive collection.

You see, we shared a special bond that made Harry a contemporary, a friend and, in many ways, a second father, enriching our lives through his memory.

Mel Adler
Smithtown, NY
May 22, 2018

Suggested Reading

Albom, M. *Tuesdays with Morrie*. New York, NY: Doubleday, 1997.

Abrams, R. *When Parents Die: Learning to Live with the Loss of a Parent*. New York: NY: Routledge, 1999.

Attig, T. *The Heart of Grief: Death and the Search for Lasting Love*. New York, NY: Oxford University Press, 2000.

_____. *How We Grieve: Relearning the World*. New York, NY: Oxford University Press, 1996.

Barthes, R. *Mourning Diary*. R. Howard, tr. New York, NY: Hill and Wang, 2009.

Berger, S. A. *The Five Ways We Grieve: Finding Your Personal Path to Healing after the Loss of a Loved One*. Boston, MA: Trumpeter, 2009.

Blackman, S. *Graceful Exits: How Great Beings Die*. Boston, MA: Shambhala, 2005.

Bonanno, G. A. *The Other Side of Sadness*. New York, NY: Basic Books, 2009.

Dass, R. *Still Here: Embracing Aging, Changing and Dying*. New York, NY: Riverhead Books, 2000.

Dimidjian, V. J., *Journeying East: Conversations on Aging and Dying*. Berkeley, CA: Parallax Press, 2004.

Doore, G., ed. *What Survives? Contemporary Explorations of Life After Death*. Los Angeles: Jeremy P. Tarcher, Inc. 1990.

Epstein, R., ed. *Dreams Wander On: Death Awareness Haiku*. Baltimore, MD: The Modern English Tanka Press, 2011.

_____. *The Temple Bell Stops: Contemporary Poems of Grief, Loss and Change*. Baltimore, MD: The Modern English Tanka Press, 2012.

Halifax, J. *Being with Dying: Cultivating Compassion and Fearlessness in the Presence of Death*. Boston: Shambhala, 2009.

Hickman, M. W. *Healing After Loss: Daily Meditations for Working through Grief*. New York, NY: William Morrow, 2002.

High, G. *The Window that Closes*. Arlington, VA: Turtle Light Press, 2012.

Knopfler, C. *I am Still Here: My Mother's Voice*. Bloomington, IN: Author House, 2007.

Konigsberg, R. Davis. *The Truth about Grief: The Myth of Its Five Stages and the New Science of Loss*. New York, NY: Simon & Schuster, 2011.

Krishnamurti, J. *On Living and Dying*. Sandpoint, ID: Morning Light Press, 2004.

Kubler-Ross, E. and Kessler, D. *On Grief and Grieving: Finding the Meaning of Grief through the Five Stages of Loss*. New York, NY: Scribner, 2005.

Kumar, S. M. *Grieving Mindfully: A Compassionate and Spiritual Guide to Coping with Loss*. Oakland, CA. New Harbinger, 2007.

_____. *Mindfulness for Prolonged Grief: A Guide to Healing after Loss When Anxiety, Depression and Anger Won't Go Away*. Oakland, CA: New Harbinger, 2013.

Levine, S. *A Year to Live*. New York, NY: Bell Tower, 1997.

_____. *Healing into Life and Death*. New York, NY: Anchor, 1989.

_____. *Who Dies? An Investigation into Conscious Living and Conscious Dying*. New York, NY: Anchor, 1989.

_____. *Unattended Sorrow: Recovering from Loss and Reviving the Heart*. Emmaus, PA: Rodale, 2005.

Lewis, C. S. *A Grief Observed*. New York, NY: Harper and Row, 1952.

Lief, J. L. *Making Friends with Death: A Buddhist Guide to Encountering Mortality*. Boston, MA: Shambhala, 2001.

Morinaga, S. *Novice to Master: An Ongoing Lesson in the Extent of My Own Stupidity*. B. A. Yamakawa, tr. Boston, MA: Wisdom Publications, 2004.

Myers, E. *When Parents Die*. New York, NY: Penguin Books, 1986.

Nyx, I. B. *Small Clouds: In Memory of Jane Reichhold 1937-2016*. Castle Valley, UT: CreateSpace, 2017.

Prend, A. D. *Transcending Loss: Understanding the Lifelong Impact of Grief and How to Make it Meaningful*. New York, NY: Berkley Books, 1997.

Rilke, R. M. *Letters on Life*. U. Baer, ed. & tr. New York, NY: Modern Library, 2006.

Schacter-Shalomi, Z. and Miller, R. S. *From Age-ing to Sage-ing: A profound New Vision of Growing Older*. New York, NY: Grand Central Publishing, 1997.

Schwartz, M. *Morrie in His Own Words*. New York, NY: Walker and Company, 1996.

Sharp, J. *Living Our Dying: A Way to the Sacred in Everyday Life*. New York, NY: Hyperion, 1996.

Shields, D. and Morrow, B., eds. *The Inevitable: Contemporary Writers Confront Death*. New York, NY: W. W. Norton, 2011.

Staudacher, C. *Beyond Grief: A Guide for Recovering from the Death of a Loved One*. Oakland, CA: New Harbinger, 1987.

Stearns, A. K. *Living through Personal Crisis*. New York, NY: Ballantine, 1984.

Umberson, D. *Death of a Parent: Transition to a New Identity*. New York, NY: Cambridge University Press, 2003.

Weenolsen, P. *The Art of Dying: How to Leave This World with Dignity and Grace, at Peace with Yourself and Your Loved Ones*. New York, NY: St. Martin's Press, 1996.

www.ingramcontent.com/pod-product-compliance
Lightning Source LLC
Chambersburg PA
CBHW071415090426
42737CB00011B/1467